isaac julien

MINIGRAPHS is a series of publications developed by ellipsis and Film and Video Umbrella devoted to contemporary artists from Britain who work primarily in the area of film and video. The series builds on a previous partnership in which ellipsis, as publishers, and Film and Video Umbrella, as project producers, joined forces to release a number of innovative digital art works, packaged as a CD-ROM with an accompanying book, on the label ●●●electric art. These new publications, while linking with 'Film and Video Artists on Tour', a programme of public presentations by each of the featured artists, are nevertheless designed to stand on their own, offering a concise and illuminating overview of the artists' influences and preoccupations and highlighting the growing interest in film and video within contemporary visual art.

We would like to thank the Arts Council of England for their ongoing support of this initiative.

Tom Neville, ●●●ellipsis
Steven Bode, Film and Video Umbrella

isaac julien

with essays by kobena mercer and chris darke

●●●ellipsis

First published 2001 by

●●● ellipsis

2 Rufus Street

London N1 6PE

EMAIL ...@ellipsis.co.uk

www.ellipsis.com

A collaboration with Film and Video Umbrella, published to accompany the
Film and Video Umbrella touring project 'Film and Video Artists on Tour'

This publication was supported by the Arts Council of England

ISBN 1 84166 073 6

Design by Claudia Schenk

Printed and bound in Great Britain by Cambrian Printers

●●● ellipsis is a trademark of Ellipsis London Limited

British Library Cataloguing in Publication Data: a CIP record for this
publication is available from the British Library

For a copy of the Ellipsis catalogue or information on special quantity
orders of Ellipsis books please contact sales on
020 7739 3157 or sales@ellipsis.co.uk

avid iconographies 7
territories 22
looking for langston 24
undressing icons 28
young soul rebels 36
the attendant 40
frantz fanon: black skin, white mask 44
trussed 48
fanon S.A. 52
three 54
the conservator's dream 60
the long road to mazatlán 62
vagabondia 70
territories: the tell-tale trajectory of isaac julien 75
lists 82
picture index 88

contents

avid iconographies
kobena mercer

Isaac Julien has created a body of work that enters into the phantasy spaces of the public sphere. 'I use the construction of iconic figures', he says, 'as a way for me to seduce audiences into witnessing something that may surprise them.'[1]

Of all the elements involved, including colour, sound, editing and composition, the figurative vocabularies of narrative and iconography are important to Isaac Julien's artistic practice because this is where his stylistic choices are in contact with the damp patches and dark corners of the culture's collective imagination. Viewing his work in film, video and installation, the experience is one in which the dream-like quality of the image flow induces a luxurious mood of 'drift'. In this condition of critical reverie, which feels at once 'transgressive and hallucinatory',[2] thoughts and sensations are directed by a poetic touch that loosens the stream of semiotic material from rigid adherence to sedimented conventions. Amid the flow, there are sharp moments felt as a piercing of the commonplace which create a 'punctum' – a moment of surprise offset by the holding environment of the surrounding pictorial narrative. The slow-motion sequences in *Territories* (1984), which interrupt the newsreel footage – like the chorus of angels in *Looking for Langston* (1989), who provide the 'studium' to the dream sequence that takes place on the Norfolk fen – reveal such moments when Julien's film practice choreographs an art of surprise.

One of the undercurrents to the major themes explored across different genres, from 1980s film and video work in *Young Soul Rebels* (1991) and *This Is Not an AIDS Advertisement* (1987) to 1990s performance and installation in *Undressing icons* (1990-91) and *Trussed* (1996), is the recurring motif of the interracial male couple. In fact, this emblematic device is often implicated in those moments of puncture and repair – the killer's glance at the black male body in the shower, and then Caz and Billibud playing records in the bedroom scene in *Young Soul Rebels* – which reveal something distinctive about Isaac Julien's expressive standpoint as a whole.

Although its presence as a signature motif could be taken as indexical evidence of Isaac's innermost desires, such a haplessly biographical reading would fail to explain why the visual trope of interracial coupling features fairly repeatedly in films by Rainer Werner Fassbinder, in photographs by Robert Mapplethorpe and George Platt Lynes, in paintings by Edward Burra, Glynn Philpot and Duncan Grant, or in literary texts by Ronald Firbank and James Baldwin. What is glimpsed through some of the portals opened by the expressive handling of the trope in Isaac Julien's work suggests something interesting about his artistic relationship to the archival relations of the Western canon. When the use of 'style' cuts an opening into the closed codes of a culture, and an artist is said to touch upon a nerve, making a mark that alters habitual ways of seeing, you could say that such practices involve a 'turn', or a 'swerve' in Isaac Julien's case. Elements previously found or fixed in one code or tradition are freed up to travel through unexpected conduits and passageways, along the lines of the trickster's tap-dance through Sir John Soane's Museum in *Vagabondia* (2000). The stylistic choices involved in Julien's characteristic handling of highly charged representations seem to lift whole clusters of cultural signage out of their given anchoring points into an intertextual flow or streaming which is then 'led astray' to fresh connective possibilities.

•••

John Goto's image showing Isaac standing beside the marble effigy of T E Lawrence in the National Portrait Gallery evokes the archival realm explored in the trilogy that comprises *Vagabondia*, *Three (The Conservator's Dream)* (1996–99) and the video, *The Attendant* (1993). John Goto's photograph reveals Julien's chosen relation to the archive as a place for a practice of critique that exhibits a careful rather than confrontational relation to the other who is discovered in the spaces of cultural memory. Isaac's proximity to the sculptural sarcophagus calls to mind his strangely funereal self-portrayal where, in the manner of James VanDerZee's *Harlem Book of the Dead* (1943), he placed himself in a coffin in *Looking for Langston*. Was it an act of identification with the lost object that the film's narrative quest was looking for? What is the romance of the ghost that presides over this scene of creative discovery?

•••

When I first saw the photograph from the British Museum's ethnographic archive (nineteenth-century, anon.) depicting a St Sebastian scene in a studio that seemed designed for anthropometric measurement, I thought I was looking at an out-take from *The Attendant*. Underlining the view that 'a photograph can seduce us by inviting us to create a meaning or narrative for it',[3] my feeling was that this anonymous image nonetheless transmitted a residue of energy in its own right. Perhaps the optical

engineers of the colonial gaze had nothing more to do on a Thursday afternoon during the rainy season. Even if it were possible to recover its originating 'intention', the agency of the image had activated a receptive capacity in which the beholder was implicated in the libidinal imprint left behind by someone else who was doing the desiring. In the face of Eros, identity can be a matter of careful indifference. In my encounter with the archival oddity, the icon was looking back at me: I had been cruised by an image on 'one of those rare and wonderful days when two strangers come together in deliberate mutual ignorance of each other …'[4]

Iconographies have a life of their own. Artists and authors come and go through the code, leaving individual imprints of the investments they bring to a particular motif, creating stylistic variation within any given tradition, period, or paradigm along the way. Or as Orson Welles once put it, 'There shouldn't be artists: just their works.'

What is significant about the conceptual basis of *The Attendant* as a film-essay is not so much that topical 'issues' of sexual and civil liberty were taken as subjects for a stylistic treatment – based on a pictorial reference to Françoise-August Biard's academic painting, *Slaves off the Coast of Africa* (1833) – but that the video's perverse copy provided the starting point for a process of 'translation' in which iconographic elements were systematically led astray.

Located in Wilberforce House in Hull as a museum artefact of the Abolitionist movement, Biard's master text suddenly yields to a strangely sado-masochistic subtext. The 'punctum' has already been delivered, for the film's very premise posits previously unlinked correspondences in the image worlds of anti-slavery and perverse sexuality. With his initial background as a painting student at St Martin's School of Art, Julien's choice of art-historical reference points can be situated among such projects of critical revision as Fred Wilson's *Mining the Museum* (1992) and Rene Green's *Bequest* (1992), or the version of William Theed's personification of Africa in the Royal Albert Memorial in Hyde Park that his contemporary Keith Piper quoted in *Allegory* (1982). Julien's film work has crossed paths with this trajectory in a way that distinguishes his standpoint as a practice of querying. *The Attendant* is a work of connective 'translation' carefully embodied by actor Thomas Baptise, who personifies a museum guard, as in Fred Wilson's *Guarded View* (1991). His surprising encounter with the leather-wearing gallery visitor induces a satin-clad Eros to make a pixellated appearance, shooting arrows of desire. It is not so much a question of labelling it queer or post-colonial, which it is, but of getting inside the diagonal moves whereby Isaac Julien's critical outlook and connective procedures resonate with Michel Foucault's view that,

> Homosexuality is a historic occasion to reopen affective
> and relational virtualities, not so much through the intrinsic
> qualities of the homosexual but because of the 'slantwise'
> position of the latter, as it were, the diagonal lines he can
> lay out in the social fabric allow these virtualities to come
> to light.[5]

•••

The Attendant opens a portal to the Black Atlantic image world of *The Deluge* by Turner, which depicts an interracial couple in the foreground to an apocalyptic scene of the Biblical flood, evoking the Romantic sublime. As an image of boundary-crossing in a symbolic universe where social identities are held to be defined by clear separations, the trope of the interracial couple is over-saturated with emotive associations. It is a visual cliché of the modern imagination in which the double contrast of sexual and cultural difference, thrown into relief by the chromatic contrast of 'race', makes it an irresistible attractor to an either/or way of seeing and thinking. The semantic coupling of 'the black man' and 'the white woman' seems always to be already full to bursting with explosive extremes of horror and wonder, terror and utopia, love and hate, gurgling beneath the hackneyed encoding of ebony and ivory's mutually forbidden fruit. As oceanic dissolution reveals the Black Atlantic as a space where terror and beauty merge, as in Géricault's *Raft of the Medusa* (1819), art shows how deeply abstract notions of 'race' and nation were given form by an optical trope of extreme contrast. Representations of Europe and Africa were reduced to 'opposites' in a visual world of antithesis where, perversely enough, the paradoxical rule is that opposites attract.

The 'inter' in interracial often interrupts or intervenes in the anchoring points of a dichotomy which is hetero-tropic, or other-directed, in its need for clear-cut boundaries. The homo-tropic realm of same-sex desire, on the

other hand, 'presupposes a desiring subject for whom the antagonism between the different and the same no longer exists.'[6]

We see such a homo-tropic dimension in Charles Cordier's *Fraternité (Aimez-vous les autres)*, which portrays two cherubs meeting in a kiss to commemorate the abolition of the Atlantic slave trade. The sculpture's avowed declaration of equality is strangely belied by the chromatic polarity of black stone and white marble, which implies a 'separate but equal' belief in absolute alterity. Cordier's allegory starts to prevaricate around the spectre of 'homoness': a quality of strangeness-in-sameness that denatures the normative rules of representation. His cherubim are coupled in an interplay of uncanny similitude and vivid contrast in which their interdependent identities are entangled *in extremis*.

The homo-tropic view also brings out of the archive a sub-genre of punishment scenes in Abolitionist paintings such as Marcel Verdier's *Châtiment des quatre piquets dans les colonies*, which depicts a naked black slave who is about to be whipped while the plantation owner and his family behold the spectacle of cruelty. By virtue of slantwise connections that reveal hidden layers to the master/slave dialectic, the violent extremes played out in the periphery betray their affinity to the founding texts of modern civility. Robinson Crusoe and Man Friday shared an intimacy in Daniel Defoe's story that was matched only by the barely sublimated homoerotic attraction that permeates Mark Twain's tale of the homosocial bond between Huckleberry Finn and Nigger Jim.

•••

Querying the canon acts upon the perverse, the inverse, and the reverse, as key terms in the 'swerve' of contemporary critical revision. It can be seen in the photographic sketch, *White Bouquet* by Nigerian-British artist Rotimi Fani-Kayode (1955–89), which offers a detranslated diagram of Manet's *Olympia* (1863) that reverses each of the dichotomies on which the confrontational shock of the master text depended.

Lorraine O'Grady's image-text work, *The Flowers of Good and Evil* (1996–99), explores similar scenes of entanglement. Charles Baudelaire's lover Jeanne Duvall, a mixed-race woman born in the French West Indies and who died in France, left behind a myth of the Black Venus. Highlighted in a novella by Angela Carter, Duvall also appears eyeless in a portrait by Edouard Manet, Baudelaire's *Mistress Reclining* (1862), and in the detail of Gustave Courbet's *The Artist's Studio* (1885), her fleeting presence as Baudelaire's 'black swan' is both acknowledged and erased.[7] Art history thus discovers black-diaspora subjects in trans-Atlantic spaces – Wilson the model who posed for George Dawe and Benjamin Haydon in London circa 1810, Joseph in

Géricault's portrait studies, or the dancer Chocolat in Toulouse Lautrec's drawings – who were already there in the imaginary institutions of the modern visual world, complicating its genealogies.[8]

Differencing the canon, Julien's homo-tropic practice of revision unearths zones of cross-cultural entanglement across Europe, Africa, the Caribbean, and America which reveal sexuality as a 'sticky' membrane of interaction, whether actual or imaginative. The sub-Orientalist strand of interracial lesbian coupling, seen in *Les Amis* by Jules-Robert August, or *The Victory of Faith* (1891) by St George Hare, is merely another portal into the realm of public fantasy opened up by the perverse turn.

'The studium is ultimately always coded', wrote Barthes, 'the punctum is not.' The interracial trope makes a sudden appearance in *Camera Lucida*, which is richly populated with photographs of blacks. Barthes continues: 'Nadar, in his time (1882), photographed Savorganan de Brazza between two young blacks dressed as French sailors; one of the two boys, oddly, has rested his hand on Brazza's thigh; this incongruous gesture is bound to arrest my gaze, to constitute a punctum. And yet it is not one [...] The punctum for me ... is the second boy's crossed arms.'[9] The object of attention belongs to the archival studio portraits of the nineteenth-century cult of male friendship associated with Walt Whitman (which calls to mind that the interracial trope in David Hockney's work is set in the Arab world of Cavafy); but the quality of Barthes' attention reveals 'race' as strangely central to the visual histories of modernity. Was it a kind of over-identification with the 'other' that led Barthes to misidentify his own ancestors in the James VanDerZee *Family Portrait* (1926), or to somehow 'magnify' the young black soldier on the *Paris Match* cover who lies at the conclusion of *Mythologies*?

•••

What would account for the fascination that images of interracial coupling exert?

Taken as a lens on to an interactive history of the different cultures brought together in Black Atlantic modernity, the trope acts as a *fascinum* for the gaze by virtue of its dynamic quality of oscillation. The graphic polarity of the black/white contrast invites the eye to oscillate between the plural meanings that arise out of the sign's connotative extremes. In a social world that aspired to the discipline of clear-cut separations, interracial coupling was not in itself transgressive, but revealed an 'idea' of boundary crossing in which sexuality was both dreaded and desired as the most intimate point of contact among the cultural differences held in place by the political fiction of 'race'. An image of a European woman and an African man together was rarely allowed to be just that – a picture of a couple – because where each identity was obliged to represent some larger abstraction, his 'race' against her 'sex', as it were, the notion that coupling brings together two halves to form a whole was constantly at risk of being torn apart by the threat of mutual antagonism between two opposite extremes. The lure of dynamic oscillation thus animates the ambivalence found in the strange logic of sameness whereby images which once incited the segregationist imagination with printed handbills depicting an interracial kiss during America's Jim Crow era were virtually identical to the images that sought to embody an egalitarian ideal of integration in the public sphere of modern liberal politics.

•••

Twentieth-century cinema was punctuated by an arc that enjoined the violent confusion acted out in the 'Gus chase' sequence of D W Griffith's *The Birth of a Nation* (1915), which imagined miscegenation as the total annihilation of separate ethnicities, to the platitudes of tolerance and reconciliation put forward in 'reply' by *Guess Who's Coming To Dinner* (1967). But whereas the prohibition on heterosexual fusions was driven by anxieties over progeniture that were bound up with the drama of the mixed-race child, which was an underlying theme of problem-oriented 'race' films in 1940s American cinema such as *Pinkie* and *Lost Boundaries*, it would be misleading to suppose that homo couplings were simply excluded from the algebra of interracial iconography. The four-square matrix that paired Dorothy Dandridge and James Mason as one taboo coupling alongside the alternate pairing formed by Joan Fontaine and Harry Belafonte in *Islands in the Sun* (1957), merely disclosed the hetero or other-directed axes of identification and desire that were merged by sameness in the intense homosocial bonding of *The Defiant Ones* (1958), in which Sidney Poitier and Tony Curtis 'begin as enemies in a jam and end as buddies in each other's arms after Tony gives up a white woman and freedom to save Sidney's life.'[10] In fact, the *pietà* at the film's ending, which actually places Poitier in a relation of mothering to Curtis, anticipates the underlying ethos of the 1980s genre of interracial buddy movies whose 'odd couplings' rely on

the frisson of homoerotic attraction that has to be managed by the storyline so that the homosocial does not suddenly give in to the homosexual (except as a joke).

What would it take to tamper with a code like that? Produced in a period when *My Beautiful Laundrette* (1985) brought a twist to the kitchen-sink realism of the post-war paradigm, substituting an Asian entrepeneur and an English skinhead to personify a divided nation, of which Noel Coward once quipped, 'I am England and England is me – we have a love-hate relationship with each other',[11] the artistic choices involved in the making of *Looking for Langston* showed that Isaac Julien had swerved away from realism's problem-solving fixations. He had entered instead into the shadow realms of inter-cultural entanglement historically buried in the crypt of the twentieth-century avant-garde.

Looking for Langston made an imaginative 'return' to the Harlem Renaissance, querying the archival relations of the High Modernist moment of the 1920s in which the first generation of Black American artists had been buried as merely a passing vogue. Opening the codes that had closed around Langston Hughes as a canonical figure in Afro-American literature, the film put forward a reconstructive synthesis of cinematic quotation, cutting through the patina in which cultural memories of 'Harlem' had been entombed. Julien's stylistic choices lifted evidence out of the canon's crevices to reveal a scene of cosmopolitan intermingling taking place in the nocturnal spaces of a speakeasy. During the period of Primitivism and Pan-Africanism, when artists shared a mutual interest in the 'otherness' of tribal objects, the interracial networks of artworld patronage often spilled over into the realm of personal relationships. Such figures as philosopher Alain Locke and artist Carl Van Vetchen played the role of go-betweens or 'translators', connecting black artists and white patrons in a milieu in which their homosexuality was tacitly accepted as such a conduit of cultural exchange in a segregated society.[12]

The nightclub realm thus forms an archival 'studium' of surplus quotation which provides a holding environment for critical reverie: its cave-like spaces are brought alive by a flickering light that reveals Eros as a source of connective possibilities in the Orphic underworld of modernism and the modern.

•••

'Transplanted from the privacy of a book or an art gallery to a film concerned with power, voyeurism and sexual desire', Martha Gever observed, 'these iconographic representations of "the black male body" are incorporated into a more expansive context, where Julien confers on his characters the license to look and, therefore, the power to envision fantasies. In the process, he stakes the same claim for himself and, likewise, for the audiences for his film.'[13] The expansive sensation registers the lifting or loosening of heterogenous elements previously closed by the caption-points of the modern art story.

In his work of contemporary revision, Isaac Julien's style of poetic translation surpasses the technicalities of appropriation. At its core, *Looking for Langston* takes a photograph by George Platt Lynes, *Two Men, John Leaphart and Buddy McCartny*, through a stylistic treatment in which the original image and its diasporic versioning pursue a lyrical chase. Platt Lynes's photograph imbues the graphic contrast of interracial chiaroscuro with an asymmetrical oscillation, heightened by McCartny's hand on Leaphart's shoulder, which was subject to a subtle modulation under Julien's stylistic handling. By virtue of the merging skin tone of the actors in Julien's version, a strange quality of sameness reconfigures what has been erased but which is still legible. The trope travels elsewhere and resurfaces at the navel of the film work, in the dream sequence ending with Alex and Beauty entwined on the bed, where Julien transposes another nude study by Platt Lynes, depicting two men undressing while another lies on the bed, into the iconographic register of the interracial code.

•••

Paul Colin and Josephine Baker, like Nancy Cunard and Henry Crowder, epitomised hetero entanglements in modernist negrophilia. In the work of Edward Burra, the enjoyment of difference for its own sake led to a homo-tropic emphasis on sameness. The two black shoremen in *Market Day* (1926) form a queer sort of couple, as do the two men in *Harlem* (1934) pictured on the street in front of a Chinese restaurant, where the one in the raincoat with the exaggerated posterior has his cigar-holding hand gesturing towards the other man's crotch.

Isaac Julien's ability to imaginatively reoccupy the pictorial spaces of Glynn Philpot, Duncan Grant and other Bloomsbury modernists cuts a swathe into the archive, revealing capillaries of influence that cut across the visual cultures of the twentieth century. 'We look for Langston, but we discover Isaac',[14] and yet we also find, in his work of diaspora imag-

ination, that the ancestors one encounters in modernism's caverns do not always have an identity that was already known in advance. Quoting Toni Morrison and Maya Deren in an equal measure of antiphony, *Looking for Langston*'s filmic ancestry can be traced back to the moment when the English avant-garde produced *Borderline* (1930), a film directed by Kenneth MacPherson, featuring Paul Robeson and H.D., whose story turns on the relationships between two couples in an interracial pairing.[15]

•••

After 1945 it could be said that the avant-garde went through a massive disillusionment with the interracial motif, as the bleak *cinema vérité* of John Cassavettes' *Shadows* (1959) suggested that a utopian vision was no longer historically available. The post-lapsarian strand that connects Stanley Spencer's painting *Love Among the Nations* (1935) to the rather more campy polysexual cameraderie of *What I Believe* (1947–48) by Paul Cadmus, drew inspiration from the jubilant pan-sexual mingling of *The Garden of Earthly Delights* by Bosch; but the Late-Modern constellation of the interracial motif owed more to Bosch's vision of hell revisited in Alan Parker's movie *Angelheart* (1986).

In the film cycle bookended by Neil Jordan's *Mona Lisa* (1985) and *The Crying Game* (1993), which would include such works as Spike Lee's *Jungle Fever* (1992) and Mira Nair's *Missisippi Masala* (1993), what accentuates the tragic version of interracial coupling is a double-bind of loving the alien with divided loyalties and no exit. This was also one of Fassbinder's themes – highlighted in *Fear Eats the Soul* (1973) – suggesting that gay/straight distinctions matter less to the ethics of inter-cultural ambivalence than the cultivation of an enjoyment of difference, or heterophilia, which is inscribed in the hybrid 'drift' of Colin McInnes's Notting Hill or the East Village worlds of Audre Lorde and Samuel Delaney in the 1950s and 1960s.[16]

Thinking of how such influences were available to the context of choice in which Isaac Julien arrived at his index of stylistic references, it is significant that his choices refract upon the post-colonial aspects of London's heteropolis. The city's migrant flows, seeping into the Powis Square locale of *Performance* (1970), and across the interracial pairings hovering above the East End in Gilbert and George's photo piece *Fair Play* (1991), have played an important part in shaping Julien's 'creole' outlook. His insights into the interplay of power and transgression are wrought from chances taken and choices made in the spatial discrepancies found in the city's unexpected routes and passages.

The superimposed pan shot of the policeman's gaze that meets Pedro's in *Territories*, like the sharp rotary swerve of the white man's gaze that breaks contact as the black boy enters the bar in *Looking for Langston*, produces moments that also occur in the documentary work – such as when 'Fanon' turns away from the boys kissing in the background in *Frantz Fanon: Black Skin, White Masks* (1995–96) – which puncture and deflate the affective extremity played out in the iconography of interracial relationships.

The soft focus of Mapplethorpe's *Abbrachio* is strangely at odds with the clinical precision of epidermal separation seen in his double portrait of Ken Moody and Robert Sherman (1984). Whether this sentimental exception, marked by a rococo title, was implicated in the twists and turns of Mapplethorpe's relationship with boyfriend Milton Moore, who is forever known as *Man in a Polyester Suit* (1980), is not for us to say, other than to observe the contrast between his binary sensorium, which is split off into manichean division, and the melancholy intelligence of Julien's image world, in which a tolerance for ambiguity has created a fluid sensibility that enjoys sumptuous surprises more than scary shock effects.

• • •

The group portrait of Isaac with Jimmy Somerville and Derek Jarman on a demonstration against Clause 28 in the 1980s makes me think how the giddy '60s excitement of the inter-racial fashion photography seen in magazines such as *Nova* gave way to the arch severity of the subcultures styled by Ray Petrie in *The Face* and other magazines, insofar as magazines provide an index of visual culture's slow fade into multicultural 'drift' as a norm of modern life. Playing with the iconography of the cowboy in *The Long Road to Mazatlán* (1999), with the 'care' shown to his pictorial reference points as a consistent feature of his imagistic or aestheticist bent, there is a camp quality to some of Isaac's choices, such as the selection of Tom of Finland drawings that appear in the background to *The Attendant*.

There is a perverse levity to Isaac Julien's translation of the *pietà* in *Trussed*, but not the evasive self-protecting irony associated with embarrassment. Without pathos either, the quality of cathexis imparted to the icon lifts it out of stasis, into an associative flow that leaks into wider

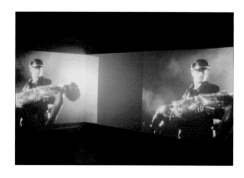

spaces of dissemination by virtue of its translation through the 'perverse dynamic' that enlivens the interracial motif.[17]

Isaac Julien's critical vision accomplishes a quality of 'aliveness' in contemporary art. It would seem to be heightened by a chosen proximity to images of dying and fading, as they arise in such moments as when Langston Hughes, reading a poem on American television, appears and then suddenly fades out into the monochrome pulse of the edit. There is avidity in this elliptical relation to the image which comes near to the rituals of dying without being afraid of the nothingness that images stand in for. As an artist trusts his or her audiences to follow through some of the portals opened up by their practice, being led astray by the creative errancy of Isaac Julien's aesthetic means staying true to a view he expressed at the outset of his career, that 'there exist multiple identities which should challenge with passion and beauty the previously static order.'[18]

NOTES

1 Erika Muhammed, 'Reel Stories: Isaac Julien', *Index*, June/July 2000, page 92

2 David Dietcher, 'A Lovesome Thing: The Film Art of Isaac Julien', in Amada Cruz *et al*, *The Film Art of Isaac Julien*, Center for Curatorial Studies, Bard College, Annandale-on-Hudson 2000, page 15

3 Chris Wright, 'Being Lead Astray', in Ruth Charity (ed.), *The Impossible Science of Being: Dialogues Between Anthropology and Photography*, The Photographers' Gallery, London 1995, page 34

4 Alan Hollinghurst, *The Swimming Pool Library*, Penguin, London 1998, page 226

5 Michel Foucault, 'Friendship as a Way of Life' in Paul Rabinow (ed.), *Ethics: Subjectivity and Truth*, New Press, New York 1977, page 138

6 Leo Bersani, *Homos,* Harvard University Press, Cambridge, Mass. 1995, pages 59–60

7 Griselda Pollock, *Differencing the Canon: Feminist Desire and the Writing of Art's Histories,* Routledge, London 1999, pages 270–77; Angela Carter, *Black Venus and Other Short Stories*, Picador, London 1985

8 Works by Biard, Cordier, and Verdier, are examined in Hugh Honour (ed.), *The Image of the Black in Western Art*, volume 4, parts 1 and 2, Harvard University Press, Cambridge, Mass. 1995/Menil Collection, Houston 1989 and in Albert Boime, *The Art of Exclusion: Representing Blacks in the 19th Century,* Thames and Hudson, London 1989

9 Roland Barthes, *Camera Lucida: Reflections on Photography*, Hill & Wang, New York 1981, pages 51–53

10 Parker Tyler, *A Pictorial History of Sex in Films*, Citadel, Secaucus, New Jersey 1974, page 249

11 Quoted in Michael Bracewell, *England is Mine: Pop Life in Albion from Wilde to Goldie,* Harper Collins, London 1997, page 222

12 Steve Watson, *The Harlem Renaissance: Hub of African-American Culture, 1920–1930,*

Pantheon, New York 1995, pages 60, 96, features family trees of
relations between artists and patrons

13 Martha Gever, 'Steve McQueen', in Ian Christie and Phillip Dodd (eds.),
    Spellbound: Art and Film, Hayward Gallery, London 1996, page 98

14 Henry Louis Gates, Jr., 'The Black Man's Burden,' in Michael Warner
    (ed.), *Fear of a Queer Planet: Queer Politics and Social Theory*,
    University of Minnestoa, Minneapolis 1993, page 232

15 Richard Dyer, *Heavenly Bodies: Film Stars and Society*, Macmillan,
    London 1987, pages 130–32

16 Colin McInnes, *Out of the Way: Later Essays*, Martin Brian O'Keefe,
    London 1979; Audre Lorde, *Zami: A New Spelling of My Name*,
    Pandora, London 1982; Samuel R Delaney, *The Motion of Light on
    Water: Sex and Science Fiction Writing in the East Village, 1957–1965*,
    Arbour House, New York 1988

17 The 'perverse dynamic' is put forward by Jonathan Dollimore, *Sexual
    Dissidence: Augustine to Wilde, Freud to Foucault*, Oxford University
    Press, London 1991, and relates to Adrian Rifkin, 'Do Not Touch: Tom,
    with Sebastiano, Kant and others,' *versus* 5, 1995, pages 18–22

18 Isaac Julien, 'Aesthetics and Politics' panel with Martina Attille, Reece
    Auguiste, Peter Gidal, Mandy Merck, 'Cultural Identities,' *Undercut* 17,
    Film-Maker's Co-Op, London 1988, page 36

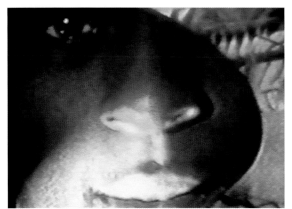

territories
1984

looking for langston

1989

undressing icons

1990–91

young soul rebels
1991

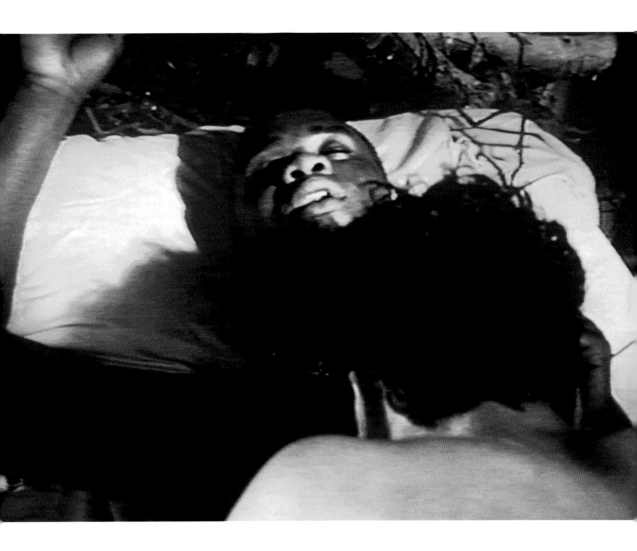

the attendant
1993

frantz fanon: black skin, white mask
a film by isaac julien and mark nash, 1995–96

trussed
1996

fanon S.A.
1997

three
1996–99

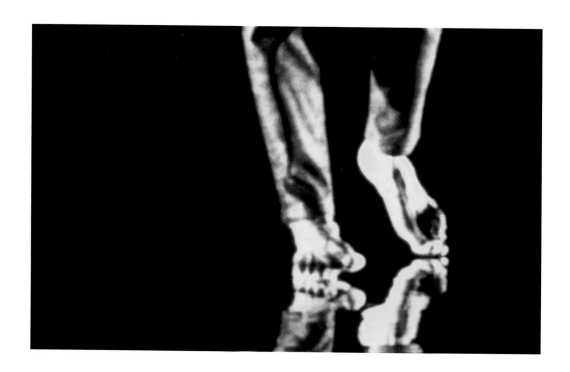

the conservator's dream
1996-1999

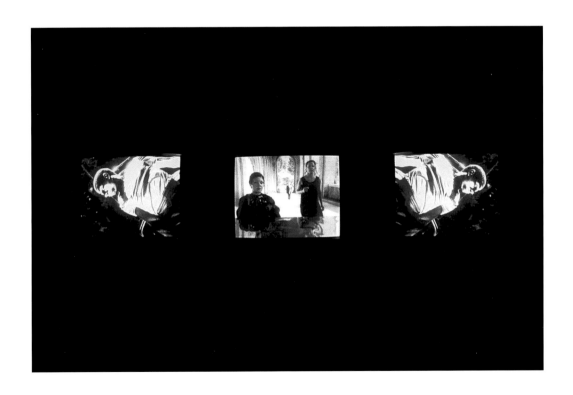

the long road to mazatlán

(director isaac julien, choreography and movement material javier de frutos) 1999

vagabondia
2000

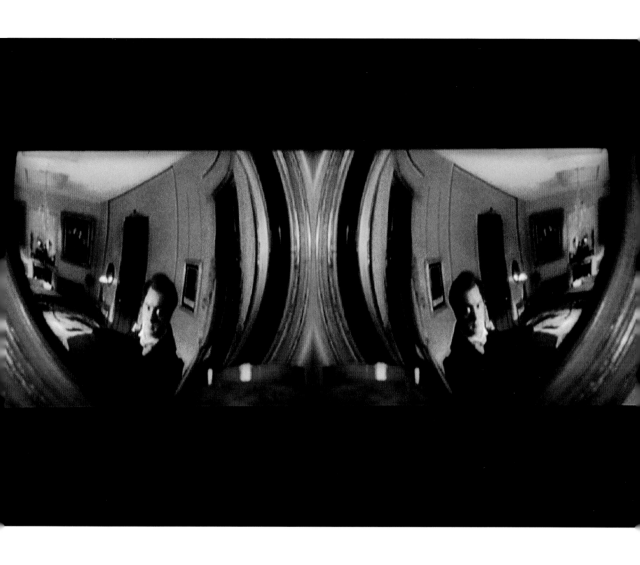

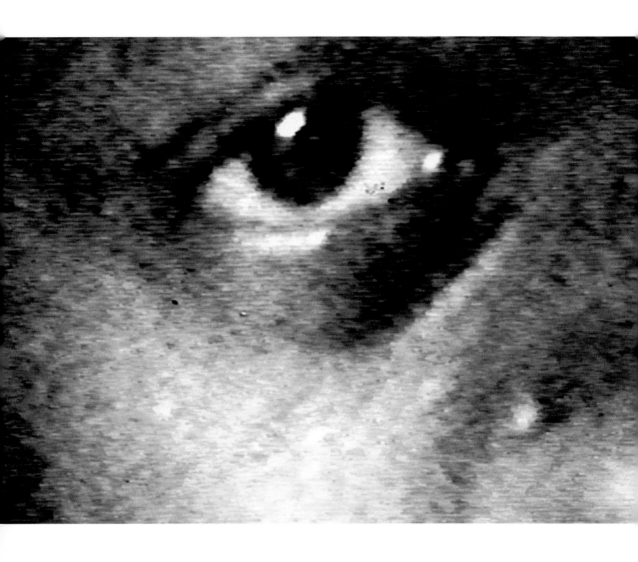

territories: the tell-tale trajectory of isaac julien

chris darke

'I cannot go into a film without seeing myself. I wait for me.
'In the interval, just before the film starts, I wait for me.'
Frantz Fanon[1]

In an interview with *Sight and Sound* magazine in 1999, Isaac Julien provocatively stated that 'the categories of fine art and cinema are out-moded ways of describing moving-image culture.' He went on to sug-gest that 'a new audience is being created [in the gallery] for something akin to the kind of experimental cinema that has been dwindling because of changes in tastes and the meagre resources given cultural film-making in this country.' Julien ended the interview in equally weighted tones of pessimism and hope: 'British art cinema is now dead, both financially and culturally, but the current interest in film in the art world supersedes this impasse.'[2] The interview was occasioned by Julien's multiple-screen moving-image installation, *Three* (1996) at the Victoria Miro Gallery and he seems to me to be a very particular case, possibly unique as a British film-maker at ease with producing work for a gallery context whose career illustrates some general tendencies of the 'moving-image culture' both in the UK and further afield. Julien has described the trajectory of his career as being similar to those of Derek Jarman, John Maybury and Steve McQueen, but a closer examination reveals a telling set of negotiations with the all-too-often short-lived possibilities for independent, interventionist film-making in Britain.

Isaac Julien is an unusual figure in British film-making for a very sim-ple reason: he's been able to keep working. A small triumph, you might think. But in many ways it is the hardest thing to achieve if you work as what was once called an 'independent' film-maker. That's to say, in the knowledge that Hollywood is not an option; that television is no longer a reliable commissioner; and that your country's own film industry has become so formulaic, conventional and conservative as to exclude any space for 'independent' or 'experimental' cinema. But when Julien started out in the early 1980s, 'independent' film-making meant some-thing different from its current connotations of Miramax and fran-chised 'cool'. It described a territory that was defined by a set of formal procedures and production arrangements that lent the term a certain, albeit subsidised, autonomy and coherence. As one of the founding members, in 1983, of the black film-making collective Sankofa, Julien (with Nadine Marsh-Edwards, Martina Attile and Maureen Black-wood) was making work that responded to a specific set of cultural, political and production circumstances. Sankofa was one of a number of workshops that emerged across the UK in the early 1980s. The incep-tion of Channel 4 in 1982, as well as the involvement of the union ACTT (the Association of Cinematography, Television and Allied Technicians), meant that the necessary combination of funding and institutional will was available to produce and broadcast material that addressed 'minority' audiences. In the case of Sankofa, as well as other workshops such as Black Audio Film Collective, there was political support in the form of the Greater London Council and its short-lived radical Labour administration which responded to demands for black representation at both political and cultural levels. Behind this political will was the desire to deal with the problems of social exclusion, racist violence and police brutality that had erupted in the uprisings of inner-city black populations in the UK during the summer of 1981.

The two major works that Sankofa produced in the early 1980s, *Territories* (1984) and *The Passion of Remembrance* (1986), were not only investigations into the material conditions of black British life but were equally intent on examining the very terms of its representation. The films were formally exploratory, placing image and sound in a contrapuntal relationship, analysing imagery drawn from mainstream media and archives, questioning documentary conventions by combining them with fictional dramatisation. They took as their starting point the understanding that there was not a 'given' visual language by which to deal with contemporary issues, not a unitary notion of black identity available, not a single account of the history of the British black experience conveniently to hand. 'We're struggling to tell a story of black people' runs the repeated voice-over refrain in *Territories*, 'A his-story, a her-story of cultural forms specific to black people'. The 'struggle' is emphasised as being one that concerned the symbolic as much as the material conditions of being black and British.

Looking again at the Sankofa films, reviewing the theoretical literature of the period and examining the circumstances in which the work emerged is a salutary and somewhat sobering experience. It's possible to have forgotten that the 1980s were, I hate to say it, a febrile and fertile time in which a sense of crisis seemed to concentrate minds wonderfully. But why does it feel so historically distant? After all, the UK is still coming to terms with being at the mercy of the unfettered, unregulated market-forces ushered in and enforced under Thatcherism. Perhaps it's because

what is visible in Sankofa's films is the last gasp of a cultural opposition that was, all too briefly, able to organise itself in the form of workshops, to take advantage of institutional outlets in the shape of Channel 4 and to theorise its practice ('Theory/Practice.' A very 1980s liaison.) in the pages of *Screen* before the journal became yet another conduit for the business of academic research assessments. In *Territories* and *The Passion of Remembrance* Sankofa succeeded in 'making the crisis speak', to use Dick Hebdige's elegantly forceful phrase – and this remains their force. The 'crisis' continues of course, barely altered but better concealed. But how can it be made to 'speak' anew, now that those former pockets of resistance have been emptied ?[3]

Writing about the black British films of the 1980s, Paul Gilroy questioned whether there was a 'base or context' for the workshop films and whether black British film culture was too dependent upon an agenda set by international film-festival circuits. But as Paul Hill has observed: 'One problem with this criticism ... is that it ignores how the "base and context" for all British film-making changed during this period and how, as a result, the film-festival circuit increased in importance for the whole of British film culture.'[4] It is illuminating to consider the shifts in 'base and context' that have happened since the 1980s. Certainly, the international film-festival circuit remains crucially important but, with the increasingly sclerotic nature of film exhibition and distribution in this country and with the greatly attenuated role of television in supporting what is now called 'cultural film' (although how 'cultural film' can be said to exist when there's hardly a 'film culture' to speak of is a question that's rarely posed), a new element has entered the equation: the gallery. In Julien's work, the institutionalised space of fine art – the gallery or the museum – becomes a theatre of desire, a repository of history, a resource of memory, as well as a space open to intervention. The museum has featured across a number of Julien's films, videos and installations. From the 1993 video *The Attendant* through to the recent installation *Vagabondia* (2000), the works attempt a 're-visioning' of the high-art context, as well as of the artefacts within it.

In his work for the gallery, Julien has taken significant steps in the developing form of the moving-image installation through his search for solutions to two problems. First, to continue to explore the tropes, themes and figures from his other work for film and television, which might generally be described as concerned with the issue of 'the look'. Second, to seek to define the distance from – as well as some of the equivalences with – *cinema* that such work calls upon. I want to put forward a hypothesis that starts with the understanding that the genre of the 'gallery film', as I have called it elsewhere, the format of multiple-projection installation, is not cinema.[5] Yes, such work increasingly involves large-scale projection (rather than single-screen monitor work) which is often regarded as 'cinematic' but that, through invoking a mobile, unseated spectator, sets it apart from cinema 'proper'. Raymond Bellour has provocatively suggested that cinema as a *dispositif* (roughly, an 'apparatus') was a form of 'installation' that worked, that became institutionalised.[6] It's no surprise, then, that the gallery should have explored alternative *dispositifs* that constantly restage the relationship between the projected image and the spectator. In the absence of the fixed and physically static spectator of cinema, and with the attenuation of the narrative imperative that necessarily follows, each installation must compensate for and emphasise its difference from the institutionalised looking of cinema, while understanding that cinema remains the horizon against which much installation work has pitted itself during the past decade.

One of the features that the gallery installation cannot replicate, and which has a lot to do with digital technology, I feel, and the extent to which the digital image emphasises surface, is the play with depth of field that cinema is not only capable of achieving but from which a refined language of cinematic *mise en scène* has been developed (from Orson Welles and John Ford via its canonical critical elucidation in the work of André Bazin, to Jean Renoir and Roberto Rossellini). It is a style that defines the classicism of film narrative. As an example of that relatively uncommon figure, the film-maker who works in the context of the gallery – Chris Marker, Chantal Ackerman, Harmony Korine and Haroun Farocki are other examples of film-makers who have pushed at the outer limits of cinema's capabilities – Julien understands that the gallery installation might be said to allegorise the current condition of cinema, while also drawing on codes and formats specific to the site of the gallery. Julien's work also exhibits an understanding that what is lost in terms of cinematic specificity in the transition to the gallery makes something else possible and he explores this in the way that his work mobilises the look of the figures in his shots, as well as the looks of his ambulant spectators. In the relative absence of cinematic 'depth' to the image, the installation flattens, fragments and multiplies both the image and, in the process, the spectator's act of looking which, rather than being absorbed into a play of depth and planes as it is with the cinematic image, is made to move across, to scan laterally, to ricochet between images.

Julien's installations, it seems to me, are quite explicit about this. They feature elements that recognise this fragmentation, this kaleidoscopic confluence of looks and gazes: the multiple split-screens and internal mirror effects of *Vagabondia*; the famous 'Are you talkin' to me?' sequence with De Niro from Scorsese's *Taxi Driver* in *The Long Road to Mazatlán* (1999) becomes the playful 'Are you lookin' at me?'. In Julien's work this also serves as an ironic reference to the trend within gallery-based moving-image installations towards a kind of 'necro-cinephilia'). But this concern with the act of looking and with the confluence of looks that cinematic spectatorship explores are long-standing features of Julien's work in which the 'look' becomes the index of desire, of conflict, of misidentification. But it must also be seen as a fundamental structuring trope of cinematic representation. Think of how 'shot/counter-shot' works in narrative cinema, the look from one character to another becoming the invisible spine of a scene, an expressive element as well as a basic structural tool. In *Territories*, for example, the 'look' is the incommensurable space between white law and black subject. It is achieved through a montage effect, that of the superimposition, given in a repeated sequence, of shots of a policeman and a young black man.

Frantz Fanon: Black Skin, White Mask (1995–96) is shot through with this repertoire of enigmatic looking, frequently breaking out of the conventions of easily stitched-together shot/counter-shot conventions and, through an effective combination of direct, frontal looks-to-camera and glancing 'unmatched' looks, converging in the territory of the spectator. One such example of this repertoire of looks is reprised several times in *Fanon* in the sequences where the film treats Fanon's time as a psychologist working in Algeria during the years of the country's liberation struggle. One of the most striking moments has two of Fanon's patients (alternately, an Algerian freedom fighter and a French soldier), Fanon himself and a hospital orderly locked in a set of looks that do not meet, that cannot meet because both patients are relating the terrifying psychic costs of oppression and resistance, in which violence means that looks cannot meet without engendering further violence.

The 'look' is a resource, as well as being an element of film grammar, of particular use to a film-maker exploring the themes of racialised and sexualised looking. Of course, the regimes of cinematic looking and their relationship to the gaze of the audience has been a core component

of psychoanalytical and feminist film theory. But in Julien's hands it also becomes a way of exploring, enhancing and defining the differences and distance between 'cinema' and the gallery film. It probably takes a film-maker to understand and fully explore the possibilities that cinema endows artists with and, in the 'other' territory of the gallery, to help define a chief characteristic of this 'other cinema' that is coming into being. In Julien's work for the gallery a sensual concern with sound, colour and movement lures the spectator into a critical engagement with the image and with the very terms of moving-image representation. Pleasure is at the heart of the politics of this work, beauty a quality of critique.

NOTES

1 *Frantz Fanon: Black Skin, White Mask* (Isaac Julien and Mark Nash, 1995–96, 70 minutes, 35 mm)

2 'In Two Worlds: Face to Interface – Isaac Julien', *Sight and Sound*, September 1999, page 33

3 Dick Hebdige in 'Recoding Narratives of Race and Nation' quoted by Kobena Mercer in *Black Film, British Cinema*, ICA Documents, 1988
At the time of writing this essay (July–August 2001), I was struck by the current face of the 'crisis' – an ongoing 'crisis' of capital, of course, but one that calls 'multiculturalism' into crisis once again. News reports resonated uncomfortably with my viewing Julien's early work with Sankofa, and particularly his pre-Sankofa video *Who Killed Colin Roach?* (1983). For example, the conflagrations between Muslim youth, police and white inhabitants of Oldham and Barnsley in July 2001 after the incursions of the racist British National Party into their neighbourhoods; the numerous reports of assaults – and in one case, the murder – of asylum seekers 'dispersed' to deprived Scottish housing estates; and an increasingly trigger-happy British police force shooting dead two innocent men, both of whom were mentally disturbed, in the space of two weeks in July and August. *Injustice*, a film detailing unexplained deaths in police custody made by the London-based group Migrant Media, has, so far, been prevented by the police from being publicly screened.

4 John Hill, *British Cinema in the 1980s: Issues and Themes*, Clarendon Press, Oxford 1999, page 238

5 Chris Darke: 'Cinema Exploded: Film, Video and the Gallery', in *Light Readings: Film Criticism and Screen Arts*, Wallflower Press, London 2000

6 Raymond Bellour, 'D'un Autre Cinema', in *Trafic* 34, 2000, pages 5–21

ISAAC JULIEN

Born 1960, London

BA Fine Art and Film, Central St Martin's School of Art and Design, London

Visiting lecturer at Harvard University and the Whitney Museum of American Art's Independent Study Program

Research Fellow, University of London, Goldsmiths' College and Oxford Brookes University

Trustee of Serpentine Gallery, London

Founder of Sankofa Film and Video Collective and founding member (with Mark Nash) of Normal Films

FILMOGRAPHY

2000   *The Long Road to Mazatlán*
         DVD; sound; 20 minutes. Single-screen version. Writer/director/producer

1996–99 *Three*
         16 mm sepia/colour film; sound; 14 minutes. Experimental fiction. Writer/director

1995–96 *Frantz Fanon: Black Skin, White Mask*, a film by Isaac Julien and Mark Nash
         35 mm colour film; sound; 73 minutes. Drama/documentary. Director

1995   *That Rush! (Williams on Limbaugh)*
         16 mm colour film; video transfer; sound; 7 minutes. Segment for *Signal to Noise* TV series. Director
         The Question of Equality (Over the Rainbow)
         Video; sound; 232 minutes (58 minutes x 4). Four-part series for US TV. Senior series producer

1994   *The Darker Side of Black*
         16 mm colour film; sound; 59 minutes. Documentary feature. Writer/director

1993   *The Attendant*
         35 mm colour film; sound; 7 minutes. Writer/director

1992   *Black and White in Colour*
         Video; sound; 126 minutes (58 minutes x 2)

1991   *Young Soul Rebels*
         35 mm colour film; sound; 105 minutes. Fiction feature. Co-writer/director
         Feel So High (1991)
         Music video for Des'ree. Writer/director

1989   *Looking for Langston*
         16 mm b/w film; sound; 40 minutes. Drama/documentary film essay. Writer/director
         Shaking the Tree
         Music video for Peter Gabriel and Youssou N'Dour for MTV. Writer/director/producer

1987   *This Is Not an AIDS Advertisement*
         Super-8 colour film; video transfer; sound; 14 minutes. Writer/director
         The Hat Videos
         Video; sound; 14 minutes. Writer/director/producer

Media Fictions

Video; sound; 12 minutes. Segment for *The Media Show*, Channel 4 TV, UK.

Writer/director

1986　*The Passion of Remembrance*

16 mm colour film; sound; 95 minutes. Fiction feature. Co-writer/director

1984　*Territories*

16 mm colour film; sound; 25 minutes. Film essay. Writer/director/producer

1983　*Who Killed Colin Roach?*

Video; sound; 45 minutes. Documentary short. Writer/director/producer

FILM/VIDEO INSTALLATIONS

2000　*Vagabondia*

Double-screen rear projection; 16 mm colour film; video transfer; sound; 7 minutes

1999　*The Long Road to Mazatlán*

Triple-screen rear projection; 16 mm sepia/colour film; video transfer; sound;
20 minutes

The Conservator's Dream

Triple-screen rear projection; 16 mm sepia/colour film; video transfer; sound;
6 minutes

Three

Single-screen rear projection; 16 mm sepia/colour film; sound; 20 minutes

1997　*Fanon S.A.*

Double-screen projection; 16 mm colour film; video transfer; sound; 10 minutes

1996　*Trussed*

Double-screen projection; 16 mm black and white film; video transfer; sound;
10 minutes

1995　*Cartooned Life*

Series of seven photographs, linotronic print

SOLO EXHIBITIONS

2001　'Isaac Julien', MIT List Visual Arts Center, Cambridge, Mass.

'The Film Art of Isaac Julien', Museum of Contemporary Art, Sydney; Blid Museet
Umeå

The Long Road to Mazatlán, Philadelphia Fabric Workshop and Museum

2000/01 *Vagabondia*, Studio Museum, Harlem, New York

The Long Road to Mazatlán, Museum of Contemporary Art, Chicago

'The Film Art of Isaac Julien', Bard Curatorial College, Annandale-on-Hudson, New
York, touring to Museum of Contemporary Art, Sydney; Blid Museet Umeå; Henie
Onstad Museum, Oslo; Yerba Buena Center, San Francisco

2000　*Cinerama* (in collaboration with Javier de Frutos), Cornerhouse, Manchester, touring
to South London Gallery

After Mazatlán, Victoria Miro Gallery, London

The Long Road to Mazatlán, Grand Arts, Kansas City

1999   The Long Road to Mazatlán, Art Pace, San Antonio, Texas

Three, Victoria Miro Gallery, London

Fanon S.A., The Arena, Oxford Brookes University

SELECTED GROUP EXHIBITIONS

2001/02 'The Short Century', Museum Villa Stuck, Munich, touring to House of World Cultures in the Martin Gropius-Bau, Berlin

'Raw', Victoria Miro Gallery, London

1999   'Retrace Your Steps', Sir John Soane's Museum, London

1998   'AIDS World', Centre d'Art Contemporain Genève, and Centro d'Arte Contemporanea Ticino

1997   'Beauty and the Beast', Banff Centre for the Arts, Vancouver

'The Look of Love', The Approach, London, touring to Southampton City Art Gallery

'Johannesburg Biennale', Johannesburg

1996   'Scream and Scream Again', Museum of Modern Art, Oxford, touring to Helsinki Museum of Contemporary Art

'Hotter than July', The Margo Leavin Gallery, Los Angeles

'British Art Now', Roslyn Oxley 9 Gallery, Sydney

'New Histories', ICA, Boston

1995   'Mirage: Enigmas of Race, Desire and Difference', ICA, London

1993   'Abject Art: Repulsion and Desire in American Art', Whitney Museum of American Art, New York

1991   'Patrick's Cabaret', Walker Art Gallery, Minneapolis

1990   'Edge 90', various sites, London and Newcastle upon Tyne

PRIZES AND AWARDS

2001   Peter S Reed Achievement Award

Eugene McDermott Award in the Arts, MIT

Shortlisted for Turner Prize

1999   Art Pace, International Artist in Residence, San Antonio

1998   Andy Warhol Foundation Award, Jerome Foundation Award, USA

1997   Pratt and Whitney Canada Grand Prize, 15th International Festival of Films on Art, for Frantz Fanon: Black Skin, White Mask

1996   Wexner Museum Fine Arts International Artist Award, Columbus, Ohio

1995   Rockefeller Humanities Fellowship Award, New York University, Center for Media, Culture and History

1993   John McKnight International Artist Award, Minneapolis

1991   Semaine de la Critique Prize, Young Soul Rebels, Cannes Film Festival

SELECTED BIBLIOGRAPHY

2001 Vasanthi Dass, 'Isaac Julien's Vagabondia', in *Isaac Julien: Vagabondia*, MIT List
   Visual Arts Center, Cambridge, Mass.
   L Wei, 'Isaac Julien at the Studio Museum in Harlem', *Art in America*, May

2000 A Cruz *et al*, *The Film Art of Isaac Julien*, Center for Curatorial Studies, Bard
   College, Annandale-on-Hudson, New York
   O Enwezor, 'Towards a Critical Cinema: The Films of Isaac Julien', *Isaac Julien*,
   Grand Arts, Kansas City, Missouri

1999 C Adair and R Burt, 'Two into the Making of Three', *Dance Theatre Journal* 15/2
   I Julien, 'In Two Worlds: An Interview with Isaac Julien', *Sight and Sound* 7
   I Julien, 'Interview', in Phyllis R Klotman and Janet K Cutler, *Struggles for
   Representation*, Indiana University Press, Bloomington, Indiana

1998 AIDS *worlds: Between Resignation and Hope*, Centre d'Art Contemporain, Geneva;
   Centro d'Arte Contemporanea, Bellinzona
   M Corris, 'Heavenly Bodies in Motion: Isaac Julien's Queer Trilogy', *Art and
   Text* 63
   M Diawara, 'Moving Company – The Second Johannesburg Biennale', *ArtForum* 7
   R Goldberg, *Performance: Live Art Since the 60s*, Thames and Hudson, London
   I Julien, 'Only Angels Have Wings' in L Cook and K Kelly (eds.), *Tracey Moffat:
   Free-Falling*, DIA Centre for The Arts, New York
   R J Powell, *Black Art and Culture in the Twentieth Century*, Thames and Hudson,
   London

1997 *Die Beute*, Edition id-Archive 17
   C Fusco, 'Visualizing Theory: An Interview with Isaac Julien', NKA, *Journal of
   Contemporary African Art* 6/7
   I Glover, 'The Look of Love: John Hansard Gallery, Southampton', *frieze* 36
   R Stam, 'Permutations of the Fanonian Gaze; Isaac Julien's Black Skin, White Mask',
   Black Renaissance/Renaissance Noire 1/2

1996 W E Crichlow, 'Popular Music, Pedagogy and Cultural Politics in the Films of Isaac
   Julien', *Discourse* 16/3
   C Elwes, 'The Big Screen', *Art Monthly* 199
   C Gaines, 'Hotter Than July', *Art and Text* 55
   b hooks, 'Thinking through Class: Paying Attention to *The Attendant*', *Reel to Real:
   Race, Sex and Class at the Movies*, Routledge, New York
   A Read, 'Film-makers' Dialogue', in *The Fact of Blackness: Frantz Fanon and Visual
   Representation*, Bay Press, Seattle
   K Silverman, 'The Ceremonial Image', in *The Threshold of the Visible World*,
   Routledge, New York

1995 D Curtis, *A Directory of British Film and Video Artists*, Arts Council of England,
   Luton
   R Grundmann, 'Black Nationhood and the Rest in the West', *Cineaste* 21/1, 2
   S Holden, 'Examining Gay Issues in Racial Settings', *New York Times*, 6 January

I Julien, 'Burning Rubber's Perfume', in J Givanni (ed.), *Remote Control*, British Film Institute, London

K Mercer, 'Busy in the Ruins of a Wretched Phantasia', in *Mirage: Enigmas of Race, Difference and Desire*, inIVA, London

B Morrow, 'The Isaac Julien Interview', *Callaloo* 18/2

1994   I Julien and J Savage, 'Queering the Pitch: A Conversation', *Critical Quarterly* 36/1

K Mercer, Welcome to the Jungle: New Positions in Black Cultural Studies, Routledge, London

1993   H L Gates, Jr, 'The Black Man's Burden', in M Warner (ed.), *Fear of a Queer Planet: Queer Politics and Social Theory*, University of Minnesota Press, Minneapolis

P Gilroy, 'Climbing the Racial Mountain: A Conversation with Isaac Julien', in *Small Acts: Thoughts on the Politics of Black Cultures*, Serpent's Tail, New York

C Houser, 'Abject', in C Houser, L C Jones, and S Taylor (eds.), *Abject Art: Repulsion and Desire in American Art*, Whitney Museum of American Art, New York

I Julien, 'Performing Sexualities: An Interview', in P Harwood and D Oswell (eds.), *Pleasure Principle, Politics, Sexuality and Ethics*, Lawrence and Wishart, London

I Julien, 'Confessions of a Snow Queen: Notes on the Making of *The Attendant*', *Cineaction!* 32

1992   H Als, 'Letters to a Soul Rebel', *Village Voice*, 7 January

D Belton, 'Isaac Julien: Britain's Leading Independent Filmmaker', *Outlook* 16

S Best, 'Displaced Desires', *Black Film Review* 7/2

I Julien, 'Black Is, Black Ain't: Notes on De-Essentializing Black Identities', in M Wallace and G Dent (eds.), *Black Popular Culture*, Bay Press, Seattle

I Julien and L Mulvey, 'Who is Speaking?: Of Nation, Community and First-Person Interview', in T Min-Ha, *Framer Framed: Film Scripts and Interviews*, Routledge, New York

J Saynar, 'Young Soul Rebels', *Interview Magazine* 22

1991   J Arroyo, 'Look Back and Talk Black: The Films of Isaac Julien', *Jump Cut* 36

M Diawara, 'The Absent One: The Avant-Garde and the Black Imaginary in *Looking For Langston*', *Wide Angle* 13/3, 4

I Julien, 'The Filmmakers' Panel', in D Petrie (ed.), *Screening Europe: Image and Identity in Contemporary European Cinema*, British Film Institute, London

I Julien and C MacCabe (eds.), *Diary of a Young Soul Rebel*, British Film Institute, London

A Taubin, 'Soul to Soul', *Sight and Sound* 1/4

1990   M Diawara, 'Black British Cinema and Identity Formation in *Territories*', *Public Culture*, 3/1

Tony Fisher, 'Isaac Julien: *Looking for Langston*', *Third Text* 12

C Fusco, 'Sankofa & Black Audio Film Collective', in R Ferguson, K Fiss, W Olander and M Tucker (eds.), *Discourses: Conversations in Postmodern Art and Culture* (Documentary Sources in Contemporary Art, Volume 3), MIT Press, Cambridge, Mass., and New Museum of Contemporary Art, New York

1989   R Auguste, with Black Audio Film Collective, 'Black Independents and Third World Cinema: The British Context', in J Pines and P Willemen (eds.), *Questions of Third Cinema*, British Film Institute, London, and Indiana University Press, Bloomington, Indiana

1988   C Fusco, *Young, Black and British: A Monograph on the Work of Sankofa Film and Video Collective and Black Audio Film Collective*, Hallwalls, Buffalo, NY

I Julien and K Mercer, 'True Confessions: A Discourse on Images of Black Male Sexuality', in R Chapman and J Rutherford (eds.), *Male Order: Unwrapping Masculinity*, Lawrence and Wishart, London

I Julien and K Mercer, 'De Margin and De Centre', *Screen* 29/4

1987   D Crimp, 'How to Have Promiscuity in an Epidemic', *October* 43

INDEX OF PICTURES

cover　　Trussed, installation view, Klemens Gasser & Tanja Grunert, Inc., New York, 2001

pp 6–7, 9　John Goto, Isaac Julien Next to T E Lawrence Effigy in National Portrait Gallery, 1999

p 8　　Vagabondia, 2000

p 9　　anon., nineteenth-century photograph, British Museum Ethnographic Collection

p 10　　The Attendant, 1993

p 11　　J M W Turner, The Deluge, 1805

p 12　　Rotimi Fani-Kayode, White Bouquet, 1987

p 14　　The Defiant Ones, film still, 1958

p 15　　Looking for Langston, Akim as fallen angel holding picture of Langston Hughes, b/w still © Sunil Gupta, Isaac Julien and Sankofa Film and Video

p 17　　George Platt Lynes, Two Men, John Leaphart and Buddy McCartny, 1938
Looking for Langston, b/w still © Sunil Gupta, Isaac Julien and Sankofa Film and Video, (left) Mathew Biadoo as Beauty and (right) Ben Ellison as Alex (Langston)
George Platt Lynes, Nudes, circa 1942
Looking for Langston, 16mm film still

p 19　　Territories, 16 mm film stills, 1984
Frantz Fanon: Black Skin, White Mask, 35 mm colour film still © Elspeth Collier, 1995–96

p 20　　Trussed, installation view, New Histories, ICA, Boston, 1996

p 21　　Trussed, 1996

pp 22–23　Territories, 16 mm film stills

p 25　　Looking for Langston, b/w still © Sunil Gupta, Isaac Julien and Sankofa Film and Video, (left) Mathew Biadoo as Beauty and (right) Ben Ellison as Alex (Langston)

p 26　　Looking for Langston, b/w still © Sunil Gupta, Isaac Julien and Sankofa Film and Video

p 27　　Looking for Langston, Akim as fallen angel holding picture of Langston Hughes, b/w still © Sunil Gupta, Isaac Julien and Sankofa Film and Video

pp 28–29　Undressing icons, performance, 'Edge 90', © Isaac Julien and locus plus:, 1990–91

pp 30–31　Undressing icons, Cibachrome prints

pp 32–33　Undressing icons, performance, 'Edge 90', © Isaac Julien and locus plus:, 1990

pp 34–35　Undressing icons, Minneapolis 1991, Patrick's Cabaret

p 37　　Young Soul Rebels, b/w still © David A Bailey, 1991; Mo Sesay (left) as Caz and Valentine Nonyela as Chris

pp 38–39　Young Soul Rebels

pp 40–44　The Attendant (1993)

p 45　　Frantz Fanon: Black Skin, White Mask, 35 mm colour film still © Elspeth Collier, 1995–96

pp 46–47　Frantz Fanon: Black Skin, White Mask, production stills, 1996

p 49　　Trussed, detail, 1st edition, photo series, 1996

pp 50–51　Trussed, installation views, Klemens Gasser & Tanja Grunert, Inc., New York, 2001

pp 52–53　Fanon S.A., installation view, The Arena, Oxford Brookes University, 1998

pp 55–57　Three (The Conservator's Dream), micro piezo prints, 16 x 25 inches

pp 58–69　Three (The Conservator's Dream), installation views, (top) MCA, Sydney, 2001 (below) Victoria Miro Gallery, 1999

p 60　　The Conservator's Dream, installation view, Victoria Miro Gallery, 1999

p 61　　The Conservator's Dream, installation view, MCA, Sydney, 2001

p 63　　The Long Road to Mazatlán, installation view, Cornerhouse, Manchester, 1999

pp 64–65　The Long Road to Mazatlán, installation view, Art Pace, Foundation for Contemporary Art, San Antonio, 1999

pp 66–67　The Long Road to Mazatlán, installation views, Art Pace, 1999

p 68　　After Mazatlán, 1999 C-type print

p 69　　After Mazatlán, photogravure images

pp 70–73　Vagabondia, installation, photographic stills

p 74　　Territories

p 77　　Territories, digital prints, 1996

p 79　　Vagabondia, installation, photographic still

p 80　　Frantz Fanon: Black Skin, White Mask, 35 mm colour film still © Elspeth Collier, 1995–96